Divorce Your

I0201879

Past

Tiffany Nation

Tiffany Nation
Chattanooga, TN
dbtoriginals@gmail.com

4-P Publishing
Chattanooga, TN 37421

Limits of Liability and Disclaimer of Warranty

The author and publisher shall not be liable for your misuse of this material. This book is strictly for informational and educational purposes. The purpose of this book is to educate. The author and publisher do not guarantee that anyone following these techniques, suggestions, tips, ideas, or strategies will become successful. This book is not intended as a substitute for the medical advice of professionals.

The author and publisher shall have neither liability nor responsibility to anyone with respect to any loss or damage caused or alleged to be caused, directly or indirectly by the information contained in this book.

All scriptures are taken from the New Living Translation Bible.

Editor: Shavonna Bush
Cover Design: Michael Simmons
Interior Design: Laura Brown

Printed in the United States of America
First Printing, 2018
ISBN 978-1-941749-87-6

Library of Congress Control Number: 2018952736

Dedication

I would like to dedicate this book to my mom and dad who stood by me during this difficult time. Also, to my sisters, who are my best friends and knew when to cheer me up. But most of all to God, who showed me grace and mercy when I didn't deserve them while showering me with love that I can always count on. Thank you, God, for showing me your unfailing love in a time when I needed it most.

Contents

CHAPTER ONE

Tuesday's Shock

My wedding on July 29th was the same day (different year) as Prince Charles and Lady Diana's. Like Diana, I had married my Prince and planned to live happily ever after with the man I loved. For a couple of years, he and I enjoyed a fairy tale life together. Then God gifted us with a surprise, a son, to make us a family. We lived in our bubble of life and happiness for almost twenty years. Even though we had our problems like every other family, I lived in my fairy tale world believing it would never end.

However, the Tuesday after Thanksgiving in 2006 was the day my world changed. A day I thought would never happen to me. I was in the kitchen preparing dinner when the phone rang. I was in the middle of chopping vegetables, so I put the knife on the cutting board, wiped my hands on the dishtowel and walked over to the wall phone.

"Hello," I answered.

What followed was something surreal. Perhaps it was something from a movie. I was completely calm as the stranger's voice on the other end said, "My name is Tom, and I have to tell you that your husband is having an affair with my wife."

I stood motionless as he continued to talk. My breathing was steady and sure as though this was no surprise; like I had expected this news when I answered the phone. In truth, it was far from anything I could have ever imagined. It felt as if I was having an outer body experience. I now realize that I was just in a severe state of shock!

Tom continued to tell me that he was bringing his daughter home when he caught the two of them in the act. He said had it not been for his daughter he would have gotten into a fight with Patrick when he found them in the bedroom.

The entire time he was venting I didn't say a word about the ordeal. I assume he expected me to go mental, holler, scream and call Patrick every curse word imaginable. At the very least to start crying and demanding to know how he could do this to me. But I didn't. I sat on the phone unable to say much until I realized Tom had stopped speaking. He wanted to know if I was going to say or do anything about the situation.

I began to slowly form sounds, and it was at that moment Tom could tell that the situation had indeed impacted me more than I let on by the silence. My voice cracked a little as I began to speak, but I quickly chocked back the tears that threatened to burst through and overtake me. I spoke in hushed tones to maintain a sense of control when I did speak.

"I appreciate your call, Tom. I had no idea, and right now Patrick isn't here. He is supposed to be home later this evening. I'm not sure how to even begin to handle this, and I know it must be hard for you, too. I don't know how long you've known, but I just found out, and I really haven't even processed this information."

Tom began to speak again, "I just wanted you to know because Patrick was talking like you already knew about the affair, but I just didn't believe that you would knowingly allow him to do something like this when there are children involved."

I spoke up at this point, "I did have my suspicions that Patrick was having an affair a few months back and I even confronted him about it. I asked him to his face directly if he was having an affair – to which Patrick replied, 'no.' I didn't press the issue as my own guilt of my own failures had already begun to flood my mind. Even though I did have my suspicions, I kept them to myself and ignored them because he had said he wasn't."

Tom was almost in tears, and I could tell that he was hurting by the affair of both our spouses. However, there were no words of comfort I could really offer him at this point, so I told him how sorry I was that he was hurting and that my husband had been part of the cause. With nothing more to say, I hung up the phone.

I stood there with my hand on the phone for what seemed hours but was only a few minutes. I was a hollow shell of a woman with no emotion or thought for the conversation that had just occurred. I heard every word and understood the implications of the words spoken by Tom, but at that moment there were no emotions inside me. There was only a sense of things I needed to do, like finishing the diner. So, I walked back to the kitchen, picked the knife back up and returned to the job of finishing the evening meal for my family.

While I prepared dinner, visions of indecent scenes of Patrick and a shadow of a woman whom I had not met began to haunt my mind. Again, the guilt of my own failure and betrayal flooded my thoughts, overwhelming me. I quickly dismissed them fearing they would overtake me. I knew my past had caught up with me, and my world was about to change, but I couldn't think about that now. I compartmentalized all the emotions of the evening and continued cooking dinner.

I didn't know how long I would have a family after the news of that afternoon came to light, as it would change the dynamics of my family. But I knew that evening I had a family for one more dinner....one more night with Patrick as my husband and Dereck, my son, and it had to be good since it would be the last.

CHAPTER TWO

Bullet to the Heart

After dinner, Patrick and Dereck went into the living room to watch TV. I joined them after cleaning the kitchen and putting away the food. The evening continued as every other night had until it was time for everyone to go to bed. Dereck went into his room while Patrick and I went into our bedroom. I shut the door and began to turn back the covers when Patrick came up behind me and touched my shoulder. It was at this moment, knowing what was to come and what was meant by his touch that everything I had been holding in came crashing around me. Tears flowed down my face. I turned to stare deep into Patrick's eyes. The burning question, "Why?" crackled out of my mouth. I didn't have to explain the question to him. I knew that he knew by the guilty expression and hurt on his face. He knew all had been exposed.

Time seemed to stand still as I sobbed. My heart was breaking, and a black hole was forming in my heart and robbing me of breath. My mind transported back to the day that I told Patrick of my affair. I wondered if his heart had been this broken. I knew he had been extremely devastated by my betrayal. I recall how I pleaded and begged for his forgiveness. Although it had taken months, he said he had forgiven me. Now I know he indeed had not. I guess he had compartmentalized like me. The words of the Bible came to mind, "you reap what you sow." The sting of truth twisted around my heart and made my betrayal hurt all the worse.

All the wrong that I had done to Patrick in my unfaithfulness became fresh again as I thought of all the hurt I had caused the man I truly loved. There were so many feelings flooding through my heart and soul that it made the tears pour from my eyes clouding my vision and I could no longer see Patrick. The once soft silent crying had now begun to turn into wailing. Patrick started to close the gap between us to hug and console me for the hurt he knew I was feeling, but I could not be comforted by him at that moment. I had to get away. So, I ran, flung open the door to the bedroom, hurried down the hall, grabbed my keys and purse, and out the door I went.

It was already close to midnight when I got into the car and drove away from our home on the mountain. I didn't know where I was going and didn't have a thought of going back to the house that night. I just knew I had to get away from Patrick and the pain that I now felt along with the pain I had caused him.

Usually, the drive off the mountain took an hour. However, that night, I think God had his angels watching over me. I don't recall how fast I was going if I ran a stop sign, traffic light or much of anything. I just remember crying, driving, and talking to God. I recall getting into the car, pulling out of the driveway and then screaming, "Why, God, why?" I choked on every tear as I screamed each word to God. I was blinking so fast just to be able to see blurs on the road because my tears streamed from my eyes like rivers blurring my vision.

I don't think I really expected God to answer audibly. However, I knew from being raised a preacher's kid that God did answer prayers, and if you listened to your spirit, you could hear him. I guess in my heart I already knew I was to blame for the heartache I now felt. I just never knew the cost and price my actions would now force me to pay. The devil counts on us to not realize the high price we will have to pay for the indulgences we allow ourselves in the present by not considering how we will have to repay the debt we will live in tomorrow.

Everything was too much to process that evening. I cried until I was exhausted. I didn't think about where I would stay after leaving the house, and I didn't know where to go. However, I knew I would not be going back that evening. I could not face Patrick knowing all the pain I had caused and my part in my family's destruction. It was crushing my heart. It was too much for me to think about and the guilt was too much for me to bear. I had to find a place to sleep, and I didn't have the money for a hotel room, so I found the church parking lot and pulled into the back, parked my car to sleep until morning.

CHAPTER THREE

What Stage is This?

In the following weeks, my world went from being shattered to being completely decimated. Patrick moved out and stopped coming over. His phone calls stopped and became texts, and even those became less. I felt lost. My family was gone, and my son had withdrawn into his own world. Even my friends and family seemed to back off because they didn't know how to act or what to say when they were around me. I couldn't blame them. How could they know what to say or how to respond when I didn't know who I was anymore? I felt like a weathered ship with no port, adrift on the sea with land visible all around but unable to find a safe haven in the midst of so many docs.

I shed many tears during these weeks of solitude. I cried out to God and wondered where He was and how He could leave me so alone. My mind was bombarded with questions like that, but my heart always told me the answer that I had always known. I was reaping what I had sown years before and that every sin has a price to pay and I was now paying the price. Some sins just take longer to catch up with you. The guilt and condemnation weighed on my heart and played like a broken record in my mind telling me over and over what a sorry person I was for betraying Patrick and starting this whole mess I now found myself in.

I knew from being raised a preacher's kid that being surrounded by church family could help if I made the choice to allow them to help. I also knew that family could help if I made the decision to swallow my pride and come clean to them about the circumstances of what was happening to me and my family. I pondered whether I wanted my family's help. If I could take swallowing my pride in having to hear my mother and my father's disappointment in their voice or worse having to look into their eyes as I told them about my betrayal. How I had not only messed my life up but the life of my son, their grandson.

I didn't know if my heart could take any more rejection. So many things had been going through my mind in the weeks since Patrick had left. The same broken record repeated in my mind, night after night. Day in and day out was the same repetition of meaningless tasks with no purpose. Each night ended the same with me crying myself to sleep and crying out to God asking for help.

Finally, a few weeks later after church, one of my friends Lynne and I were talking, and she told me about a DivorceCare©, class that I should attend. She could tell that I was apprehensive about going. However, she assured me that it was worth my time and effort to attend as it was for people in my situation who could understand exactly what I was going through. I got the information from her along with the name and contact information of the person who was teaching the DivorceCare class. I thanked her and told her I would reach out and see about enrolling. But in the back of my mind, I thought it would be a waste. Who would really understand what I was going through? Lynne meant well, but she was still married along with all my other friends. Some of my friends were already telling me to move on and acting as I should be over Patrick. But, how could I? We were married for almost twenty years, and I couldn't be expected to get over it in a matter of weeks. I wasn't built that way.

As I drove home from church, Derek and I locked eyes for a moment. I smiled softly at him as I reached over to gently rub the top of his head like I had done when he was young to reassure him that everything would be fine. However, I didn't know if things would be okay again. All I could think about during those days was how I'd ruined everything. The voices, or since I had been in church I then recognized as the devil, had been giving me an earful and I'd been listening to a lot of self-condemnation.

I thought about Derek and how he would grow up without the presence of the father in the house because of me. I thought of how I had ruined our Christmas, our family vacations, and our family in general. I thought of how Patrick and I would no longer be together when Derek got married or when Derek had his first child. It was the catalyst effect because of me and my sin. I know part of me, the rational part, kept telling me that I was not solely to blame, but the self-loathing and condemning part of me kept saying it was all my fault. With each thought, my heart became heavier and heavier, and once again my breaths became labored. From the corner of my eye, I could see Derek becoming concerned, so I had to put my best face on for his sake, at least until we got home, and I could retreat into my bedroom.

After arriving home, with my heart heavy and my breath still labored I withdrew into my room, closed my bedroom door, and let the thoughts of my sins punish me as I thought they should. I was in a prison without walls that I'd built myself. I wept silently so Derek would not hear me. The pain in my heart had grown into a black hole consuming all joy, hope, and life out of me. Guilt overwhelmed me, and it didn't matter what precipitated my betrayal so many years before. All I could see was the mess I now lived in because of the mistake, because of the decision I chose to make. That was another broken record repeating itself, why had I done that? Why had I cheated on Patrick that day?

I could list all the reasons caused by Patrick, but that wouldn't change the way things ended up, the pain and hurt I caused Patrick, my son, and the destruction of my family. I didn't feel I could live with all the pain and damage I had caused along with the continual gnawing of guilt I felt with every breath I took. So, I went to the dresser, opened the drawer where the Glock was kept and took it out. I sat down on the edge of the bed. My heart began to hurt more as I took the safety off. I silently prayed once again, "God, if you're listening, please help me I cannot take this anymore. Please forgive me for what I'm about to do. This pain is more than I can bear. I have destroyed my family. I have looked at myself in the mirror as described in James 1:23 and I'm so ugly, and selfish and I can't stand nor bear to look at that person anymore because no one would want that person."

Having said that silently, tears streaming down my face, I put the gun to my right temple closed my eyes swallowed and began to slowly pull the trigger. I was stopped by the faint knocking at my bedroom door and the soft voice of my son Derek, asking "Mommy are you okay?"

It was at that moment that I knew God existed beyond any shadow of a doubt. God heard my plea of desperation and answered through my son. I put the safety back on the Glock, put it away, ran, opened the door and gave Derek a hug. In my heart, I thanked God for answering my prayer. I thanked God for my son and for God's perfect timing. That evening when I slept, I still hurt and longed for Patrick, but this time the tears that flowed from my eyes were from a broken woman.

I was humbled and grateful that the God of the universe had heard my prayer that day, after all, I had done and how bad I had messed things up. I was overwhelmed with a sense of peace I had never known before, and I knew that God would be with me from now on as long as I surrendered to him as I had that day. With this knowledge, I closed my eyes and drifted off to sleep.

CHAPTER FOUR

Now It Hits the Fan

The next day I enrolled in the DivorceCare class determined to seek God's help after experiencing his love and peace the day before through prayer. I talked with one of the teachers of the course, June, for almost half an hour. She seemed to understand what I was going through. She told me about the class and how it was structured and gave me her number along with her email and told me to call if I needed anything or needed to talk.

The days passed quickly to my first DivorceCare class. It was like the first day of school. My heart beat fast, and my mind raced with thoughts of what the class was going to be like. I pulled into the parking lot, and the butterflies hit my stomach as I walked towards the door. I took a deep breath, put a smile on my face, opened the door and walked into class.

June greeted me and made me feel welcomed by introducing me to everyone along with the other teacher and her husband, Todd. She gave me a DivorceCare workbook, and class began. The lesson that evening touched on every feeling I had been experiencing and seemed to be speaking to every emotion I had felt in the weeks and months since Patrick left. As the class wrapped up for the evening, June and Todd went over the homework we were to do for the week.

That evening when I got home, I eagerly began to read and study my DivorceCare workbook. Everything

I'd learned that evening in class was refreshing and different from the way I had been raised to think about divorce. Being raised in the church, as I had, it was almost taboo and frowned upon to get a divorce. As a preacher's kid, my perception had been somewhat skewed and jaded, but then so was the world's view of how a Christian should act. The world had their own rules of how a Christian should behave and what a Christian should do in situations such as mine, at least this is how it was in the South where I grew up.

I knew I needed God's help to get through whatever this was with Patrick. I didn't know where I stood with him. Patrick had moved out, but when he wanted to stay the night or weekend, I would allow him back in the house thinking I was doing my Christian wifely duty. However, after my first DivorceCare class and listening to the video that evening, then coming home and diving into the lesson and homework for the week, I learned that was not how God intended love to be. I had to give Patrick tough love. I had to set boundaries for myself.

So many things were happening to me, and there were so many overwhelming feelings at different times. It was like a ball of emotions. At times I felt lonely then rejected, followed by guilt, then rage, then depression, then disgusted, and it all seemed to cycle back around. It was like a never-ending bad dream that you couldn't wake up from, and you wondered if it will ever end.

As I worked through the lesson for the week, I tried to answer the question of what stage I was in pertaining to the grief process, but I couldn't as my emotions were still too raw to process from all that had happened. However, it did give me knowledge and wisdom to be able to understand all the feelings and why I was feeling them in such repetitious cycles.

CHAPTER FIVE

Just When You Think
You Have a Handle

Over the next months as I attended DivorceCare class and worked through the workbook my relationship with God began to deepen. I started to meditate on the Scriptures, something I had never done before. I began to reflect inward and think about the verses in James 1:23-25 which says,

> "**23** For if you listen to the word and don't obey, it is like glancing at your face in a mirror. **24** You see yourself, walk away, and forget what you look like. **25** But if you look carefully into the perfect law that sets you free, and if you do what it says and don't forget what you heard, then God will bless you for doing it."

Those voices seemed to stick in my mind and resonate with me. I could visualize looking at myself in the mirror. The only problem was I didn't like what I saw because every time I looked in the mirror, I heard the voices that echoed every feeling I felt. The voices that said, *this mess was caused by you. Look at what you've done to your family. How can anybody love you? Everything you touch turns into a disaster. Everywhere you go, you just hurt people. Everyone you love gets hurt.* If that wasn't enough, the guilt turned to blame and self-loathing and then the voices would say, *maybe the world is better off without you. At least you wouldn't be hurting anyone.* Sometimes the guilt was overwhelming, and

I had to plunge it deep inside me to carry on.

In my mind, I would look at myself in the mirror and confront the ugly person I had become. Or maybe I was always this ugly but didn't realized the truth because I didn't dare to stare into the mirror that had always been there and just never recognized until now when I had to face this truth because I was left alone with no one to blame but the person I now saw in my reflection. It was a hard truth to face and one I wasn't sure a shattered shell of a person like me could handle, at least not by myself. But once again God was ready to prove himself and help me yet again. Each time I looked into that mirror as I worked through the workbook over the course of those thirteen weeks in DivorceCare Class, God was there to help me and give me peace.

I knew without God's help I was going to be a monster or worse, the ugly twisted person that I saw in the mirror who created so much chaos. I simply could not bear creating any more destruction. I especially did not know what to do or what to say when it came to Patrick. Anytime Patrick called or texted I said a prayer before I answered the phone or replied to his text. Even then I would sometimes lose it just when I thought I had a handle on things. I would have to go to God and say, "You have to help me if you want me to have the right attitude. I know you don't like the attitude I have right now, but I can't talk to Patrick unless you help me talk to him the right way. So, God, please help. Otherwise, I can't do this."

I didn't know where in the Bible to really start reading for the help I needed in addition to reading the Scriptures from my lessons in DivorceCare. So, I began to read the Book of Psalms and a chapter of Proverbs for the corresponding day of the month. I opened the Bible, and it opened to Psalms 34. Verse 18 stood out because my heart was still very much broken. It reads,

The LORD is close to the brokenhearted; he rescues those whose spirits are crushed.

I then turned to Proverbs 18 as it was the 18th day of the month and began to read. I stopped reading the chapter when I got to verse 14, and the tears started to flow again. It was as if God knew both the verses I read that day spoke directly to me. Verse 14 reads,

The spirit of a man sustains him in sickness, But as for a broken spirit, who can bear it?

I was still crying myself to sleep and crying out to God because these things do take time, and wounds don't heal overnight. Yes, God can miraculously heal a broken heart. However, most of the time God allows us to go through these difficult situations to allow us to grow and learn so that we might develop character. We don't see the change until we've gone through the transformation and we don't understand, if ever, until after we have gone through a difficulty. I believe God allows this so that we might remember the problems and challenges that the struggle will enable us to face to prepare us for the next journey of life. How we carry ourselves till we depart from this life reflects not only our character but how well we mirror our designer's beauty with the endowed potential he has given us to discover our purpose, using it to its fullest, and become his masterpieces. This takes a lifetime to master. It is a rough road to travel, but the journey is worth the adventure.

CHAPTER SIX

How Long?

Growing up in the church as I had, I thought I had a relationship with God, but I didn't. I was raised in the church, but yet I had no real relationship with God. It took Patrick leaving for me to develop a real relationship with the Father.

I would like to say I'm sorry that my divorce eventually happened. However, the truth is, I'm not. God used Patrick as a wake-up call to allow me to see I didn't have a relationship with Him. Yes, I was saved, and if I died I believed I would've gone to heaven, but I had no fruit as the Bible called it to show for the efforts I was doing. The world would've called me a Sunday Christian or might have called me a hypocrite.

By worldly standards and a worldview, I suppose you could say I was a good Christian. I went to church, paid my tithes, went to Sunday school, made sure to bake a casserole if someone died, volunteer if one was needed, and helped when I could. Despite all these outwardly appearances, I really was no different than anyone else.

Once again God intervened and allowed me to turn on the television when an evangelist named Joyce Meyer was on TV. She was talking about the *Battlefield of the Mind* and about renewing your mind. I knew about renewing your mind because I was raised in the church, but I had never heard it spoken like she talked about it. Everything she said seemed to be directed at me. It was as if she knew what I was going through. I knew there is no way this woman could know anything about me and yet everything was relevant to the situation I was facing.

My dad was a pastor, but I had never heard him preach the way this lady preached. She put things in a practical, matter of fact this is how you apply the Scripture kind of way so that you could understand it and live it. It was eye-opening to me. Then she quoted the Scripture that would be the basis and foundation of hope for me to carry me through my healing during this time. It was Jeremiah 29:11,

"For I know the plans I have for you," declares the LORD, "plans to prosper you and not to harm you, plans to give you hope and a future (NIV)"

Joyce said, "If you're listening to this, God wants you to know he has a plan for your life, and it is a good plan, plan to prosper you and give you hope. Don't listen to the lies of the enemy, the devil. He wants to steal your joy, your prosperity, and your destiny. Don't let him."

I was completely stunned and amazed. I knew God had used her to talk to me yet again. He had to be because she was on TV speaking to millions of people. However, this message seemed to be tailored fit specifically for me and the situation I found myself struggling to get through.

I'd been doing the lessons in the DivorceCare workbook, but I was struggling in my mind wondering how long it was going to take for me to find some semblance of normalcy again?

CHAPTER SEVEN

Is Anyone There?

DivorceCare class ended, and I'd learned a lot. I also learned a lot from watching Joyce Meyer, but I knew I was still just a baby so to speak. I still had a lot more to learn and digest in terms of growing up to be a mature Christian.

I was going to church regularly again and started attending Sunday school. I even joined the women's group. However, it appeared all my friends had abandoned me when Patrick left. I knew this was just my feelings getting the better of me, but they didn't call or come around like they once had before he and I separated.

It wasn't their fault, and I couldn't blame them really. It was just an unfortunate part of life that happens because most people don't know what to say or how to deal with situations like this. But it didn't help me. I really needed and wanted a human friend. Someone that I could touch and hear with my actual ears. A friend that I could talk to when I was feeling down and especially after I had spoken with Patrick because it was after his calls or the texts when I would feel very vulnerable and raw again like he had just left even though it had been months now.

I wanted to get past all these feelings and to learn from my mistakes so that I would never allow myself to make the same mistake again should Patrick, and I reconcile. However, with each passing day, it got harder and harder to believe that reconciliation was possible. My heart wanted the reconciliation because my heart still loved Patrick. I knew that love could tear down any walls and heal all wounds with time. But as the days turned into weeks and months and Patrick made no attempt to come back, I began to put up my own walls within my heart to protect it so that it would not be hurt again. At least that is what I tried to tell myself.

Just when I thought I was going to be okay, Patrick would text or call, and we would meet, or he would come over, and my hope of our reconciliation would bloom all over again. Looking back, I think Patrick may have wanted reconciliation as well but may not have known how to begin to reconcile with me with both of us hurting the way we were. Both of us were dealing with guilt from our own mistakes, and that makes for a bad reconciliation on any level.

Soren Kierkegaard said, "Life can only be understood backward, but it must be lived forwards." I understand now but didn't at the time that I was in a repeating cycle with Patrick. I repelled a lot of my friends unknowingly by continuing to put out negative energy of depression during the first few months after Patrick left. Then it became more of a moping aura rather than depression. My friends didn't want to be around that type of disparagement. But this is something you can only see in hindsight or experience when dealing with a friend that is going through it and not yourself.

So, I went to God. The DivorceCare classes had given me direction and helped me to start my growth and journey in healing. Then God intervened once again and allowed me to tune in to Joyce Meyer, and as a result, I started listening to her program in the mornings and had even ordered her book, *The Battlefield of The Mind.* I began to read it, and everything seemed to speak to me just as it had on the television.

In the book, Joyce Meyer points out how important it is to renew our minds as Christians. This is something that I had heard my father preach in church and even heard him quote the scripture from Romans 12:2,

"And be not conformed to this world: but be ye transformed by the renewing of your mind, that ye may prove what is that good, and acceptable, and perfect, will of God."

In the weeks that I had begun to listen to Joyce Meyer and read my Bible for understanding and knowledge. I began to grasp what that verse meant for the first time. The Holy Spirit allowed me to understand that I had to change the things that I thought about and what entered my mind. I had to guard my mind. Not only that but the songs that I listened to, the movies that I watched, the books that I read, the friends and the company that I kept. The Holy Spirit revealed to me that all these things were factors in the makeup of whether I produced good fruit or bad fruit. The Holy Spirit reminded me of Proverbs 23:7,

"For as he thinks in his heart, so is he..."

As I began to think about these things the Holy Spirit allowed me to understand, the enemy crept in and began to say to me, "It's not gonna kill you listen to the songs you like and watch the movies you want to watch and hang out with your friends that you've known for years." However, the Holy Spirit reminded me of the old saying one bad apple spoils the whole bunch. The Holy Spirit showed me that it takes one thought to infect your whole way of thinking for words are powerful and they are life and death. Since words begin with thoughts, every thought comes from your mind and what you put into your mind matters. So, if you are filling your mind with junk and a lot of nonsense or useless material that has no purpose to help you in your growth or edification of yourself or of others, then it is a hindrance to you and therefore has no purpose. You should consider carefully what goes into your mind because it will come out as words and words can be the most damaging things to a human soul than anything else.

Pearl Strachan Hurd said, "Handle carefully, for words have more power than atom bombs." Words have been used to stir crowds of people into motion and direct nations into action and even war. I pondered these thoughts the Holy Spirit had put into my mind and spirit as they were wisdom. I began to see how right the Holy Spirit was as I recalled many excellent speeches that stirred people to action and are still remembered to this day. Many have become national holidays we remember because of the significance of the impact they have made. No one will ever forget the horror of the Holocaust because the words Hitler used persuaded people - good people to do bad things. People still remember Dr. Martin Luther King's moving speech about the inequalities of racism and segregation. Going back even further almost 2000 years ago people still debate Jesus and the sermon on the mountain from Matthew 5:3-11, the beatitudes; whether you believe in Jesus or not seems everyone has taken something from it. They have taken it in whole or in part and used it as guidelines to live by.

I took these things to heart, and another Scripture came to mind, Ephesians 4:29,

"Let no unwholesome word proceed from your mouth, but only such a word as is good for edification according to the need of the moment, so that it will give grace to those who hear"

I knew I had not been doing that given my depressing state of mind and spirit. So, I began to ask God to help me in that area. After all, I knew from the Bible if you want a friend, you must first show yourself to be a friend, and I had not been a friend. I had only been a walking, talking negative, never-ending cycle of depression. It's no wonder I had the few friends that I did and that they stuck with me. I decided that was going to change after listening to Joyce Meyer and reading my Bible. I began to understand how my thoughts affected my words, actions, and the people around me.

CHAPTER EIGHT

The Right Attitude

I knew I had a long way to go, but I began to feel and see a brand new me when I looked in the mirror. That encouraged me and gave me more self-confidence. I wanted to change more, to become better than what I saw in the mirror when I indeed looked at myself honestly instead of through rose-colored glasses and the lies. What I wanted to believe about myself was easier to swallow at times than the hard-naked truth of what the ugliness revealed. So, I signed back up for another thirteen weeks of DivorceCare classes to make sure I really absorbed all the lessons and knowledge from the course. Because I had not asked for a divorce and I was not going to ask for a divorce, I wanted reconciliation with Patrick because I loved him. However, if he did not want to reconcile and make amends, then there was nothing I could do other than pray for him and leave it in God's hands. This is where I had to turn it over to God and allow God to heal my heart from the brokenness and scars that were left.

It is a humbling experience to come to the place of self-realization when you cannot clean up a mess that you now sit in and must pick up those pieces and relinquish them to God so that he can make a masterpiece from the broken pieces. This is where growing up in Christ takes place, and it can be painful because you can no longer wander about blissfully ignorant of things.

Now you must be responsible and accountable for actions and things that you do and how you do them.

Since I had begun to listen to Joyce Meyer a few months back and started reading her book, I learned about renewing my mind. I learned that my attitude mattered. I didn't realize there was a right way and a wrong way to do something right if you are doing something good. But attitude is the key that makes the difference of how things are received and the spirit it is received.

I had to ponder this every time I spoke to Patrick on the phone or text because I wanted to make sure that I was representing Christ to the best of my abilities and I needed the Holy Spirit to do that. Sometimes I had to pray and fast to get my thoughts together to speak to Patrick. Sure enough, my attitude wasn't right.

I would come across as a scorned woman or a rejected woman at times, and neither was someone I ever thought I would be. However, a broken heart and sleepless nights had led me to face these women in the mirror of the reality of truth, and it pained me. Pained me to the core of my existence because if they are honest with themselves, no one ever wants to think or believe they could ever truly be so ugly a person as the person staring back in a mirror of truth. That's the type of reality that tears at a person's soul the most and eats away at you bit by bit with guilt if you dwell on it too long. You see the nasty ugliness of a person you can hardly recognize but know that it is the dark, selfish nature inside that has claimed its way far too long, caring only for itself and never stopped or cared about the needs or wants of others. The desires of the flesh only feeds itself, which is why it is so painful and hard to look at know in the mirror of truth.

For I believe it is this part, the scorned and rejected woman, that came to the surface the most. That is what Patrick saw often and rejected the most in me when he came to the decision to leave. Looking and facing that truth hurts the most when I take ownership in my part of the divorce, but acknowledging my part and seeing the truth is the first step in making a change.

Other times the truth revealed that my attitude had been the woe is me or the victim attitude. The victim is the one I gravitated toward the most, and I seemed to wallow in. It was easier to deal with and accept, but I knew this wasn't the attitude that God wanted me to have. He wanted more for me, but I needed to learn to take the hard truth and learn from it. This is where I had the trouble accepting and believing his truth. I even had to talk to God about this.

I wanted to have the right attitude. I saw what the wrong attitude had done to my mother-in-law, Patrick's mom, Daisy. Daisy was married to Patrick's birth father T.J. for a short time. They divorced while Patrick was just a baby. After T.J. divorced Daisy, she became bitter and hateful through the years. She was unable to forgive T.J. for divorcing her, and that unforgiveness deepened into a hatred that oozed a toxic poison infecting every aspect of her body, mind, and soul. It had consumed her to the point that the mere mention of his name would cause Daisy to spout profanity or become so enraged that she couldn't bear to be in the presence of someone talking about him without having to leave the room. Daisy didn't realize, or maybe she did but didn't care that she exuded such acrid hate for T.J that everyone around her could feel it, coating them with its toxic venom.

I knew I didn't want to end up like that, becoming a bitter old woman eaten up and consumed with hatred for Patrick. Then alienating myself from all my friends and family because they wouldn't want to be around me spilling my venom of toxic unforgiveness onto them. A kind of grim that you can't wash off with soap and water. It must be weeded and rooted out. However, first, you must stand in the mirror of truth and be willing to face that truth head-on and change it.

I had to pray every time Patrick called or text that God would help me have the right attitude toward him. I prayed that God would allow Patrick to see His spirit in me and not myself in the call. I prayed that the Holy Spirit would bind my tongue that I might not say an inappropriate word toward him and that all my words would be directed by the Holy Spirit to bring peace and healing. This was going to be a task He would have to help me with, as I knew I didn't have the strength within myself to do it on my own. As I prayed these types of prayers, when Patrick would call or text, he and family and friends noticed the change in me. They asked what was going on with me or would tell me what an inspiration I was to them for being so positive and staying in a positive place during a time of duress.

As I heard my friends tell me they were inspired by me, I was flabbergasted. I wondered how they could be inspired by me. Did they not see how much a mess my life really was? On the inside, I was falling apart! At night sometimes, I lay in the fetal position and cried myself to sleep wondering if it was ever going to get better because all I could see when I looked into the mirror of truth was the ugliness of a person I didn't like, a person Patrick had left and a person I was desperately trying to change. That is the beauty of how God works. He takes the ugliness when we are willing to give it to Him and when we have a right heart and attitude, He gives us beauty for ashes. When we see the brokenness, the world sees the beauty God is making because of our right attitude. We often never see it until after the fact because we are in the midst of humility at its finest. God can work His best when we allow him to clean up our mess by giving Him our ashes which He makes master-pieces for the world to behold his glory.

CHAPTER NINE

Sex, Dating, Cybersex?
I Need a Dictionary!

After going through my second round of DivorceCare classes, it was clear Patrick and I were going to get a divorce because he had asked for one. I didn't want one and had not asked for it, but since he did, I began to prepare myself. I was glad for my friend Lynne who stood by me and recommended the DivorceCare classes to me. They helped me with the process of the divorce. She even went with me to the courthouse the day of the divorce.

I thought the day I found about Patrick's affair was the hardest day of my life, but that was before this day. The day I walked into court to face a judge who didn't know me or Patrick to just say we had irreconcilable differences like our marriage had meant nothing. I could feel a new wound opening over the wound I thought had healed after all the classes, the books I read, and videos I listened to from Joyce Meyer. It all seemed like it had been a waste of time now that the fresh wound appeared to be ripping my heart wide open again, as though the black abyss I thought I had escaped was back threatening to envelop me in its darkness.

I looked between Patrick and the judge as the judge asked me if there were any final words I wanted to say before he passed the judgment down. The only thing I could say in a cracked voice, trying not to cry was, "You can't make someone stay with you that doesn't want to stay with you." I turned from Patrick, not wanting him to see the tears now wailing up in my eyes. I faced the judge heard him dissolve our marriage of almost twenty years.

I couldn't get out of the courthouse fast enough, and I was ever so grateful my friend Lynne had come with me. She followed me out to the car where I quickly got in so the tears could freely flow. Lynne allowed me to cry on her shoulder while she held me. I knew my friend was silently praying for me, as I could feel the presence of the Holy Spirit's comforting warmth begin to wash over me and spread into the corners of my heart starting to make me feel whole once again.

I knew God had not abandoned me and he would never leave me. I could feel God's love and peace settling over me, and I knew all the books, videos, reading and listening to programs about the nature of God helped me learn who God was and the true nature of God. After a few minutes of crying and hugging it out, I composed myself for the drive home. I knew God would be there to help me figure things out and to help me continue to heal. Life would go on, and he had a plan for my life. His plan and purpose are always good for me; I just had to get in agreement with them.

Now, I was finally on the road to getting in agreement with His plan and purpose for my life by surrendering to His will and not mine. I looked at Lynne, smiled and thanked her for coming. Then I started the car and headed back home a single woman with my friend Lynne.

This was the beginning of a new chapter in my life that opened the door to my friends trying to set me up on dates now that I was single. I had not dated since I was a teenager. I knew things had changed. I didn't even know the rules of dating anymore.

Nowadays there is online dating, mobile phone dating, dating where girls pick up the checks and dates that are more coffee get-togethers and not so much dates. I could tell there was going to be a lot I was going to have to learn about dating in today's world. It was going to be like going through puberty again, only now I was older, didn't have the patience for it and didn't know the rules for it any better now than I did when I went through puberty the first time.

I accepted the few dates my friends set me up on because I knew they were trying to help get me moving forward with my life and to get me over Patrick. But it was scary for me to think about moving on without Patrick. I had been with him for almost half of my life. He was my best friend, and now I could no longer consider him a friend, even though we both said we would always recognize each other as friends. At first, I'm sure we would be friends but as time passed the casual texts and phone calls to say hi and stay in touch would become less and less. Then it would stop altogether as Patrick would no doubt be conflicted about talking with me when he was dating his girlfriend, and I would then become a problem for them. I would just have to make myself go on dates and learn to accept that my life now would not include him. Lucky for me, I had friends that had teenagers who were happy to give me dating tips as well as fashion advice. They helped me set up online dating accounts, create profiles, take pictures for the profiles and tell me what different things meant, especially with the emojis.

After a couple of dates, I began to feel like something was missing in the equation. I understood what the game of dating was about and realized what it was what most men were seeking when I went on these dates. Although they claimed to be seeking a relationship, it appeared to me most were only interested in the first date and what they could get out of it and nothing more. I began to question myself and whether the divorce had left me jaded at all men or just my judgment and faith in them. I also started to wonder if I could ever trust them again and wonder if any man would ever measure up to Patrick and the pedestal I now found myself placing him on.

Most people would find the situation somewhat of a conundrum. To still be in love or want a man that hurt or rejected you and yet find yourself wanting the same man in the way that I now found myself. I pondered the scenario and wondered if it was because we had been married for so long or if it was because my heart still belonged to him. After all, we had joined spirit, body, and soul and become one, as the Bible said, "...and the two shall become one."

This was such a strange new world to navigate abstaining from sex. Although I have never been an addict of drugs, I would dare to compare it to being an addict of drugs in a sense because it's not like you can put something like that back in a bottle. You can't unlearn the feelings, sensations, and memories your body has about the pleasures of sex once you have had intercourse. I can see now why God wanted it to be within the confines and sanctity of marriage and marriage alone. It was meant to be for our protection but also for our pleasure, but it is greatly distorted, misused, and abused.

Going through the DivorceCare classes, they devoted an entire chapter on single sexuality and what it meant to keep yourself pure since now you would be a single, divorced adult who had tasted and known what sex was inside a marriage. I was glad to see there was a chapter that talked about keeping yourself pure and sex outside of marriage with consequences in today's world.

I grew up as a preacher's kid, and it was very taboo to talk about sex inside of marriage let alone sex outside of marriage. I always thought there needed to be more discussion and education about the consequences and evils of sex outside of marriage because as the Bible says in John 10: 10,

> *The thief does not come except to steal, and to kill, and to destroy. I have come that they may have life, and that they may have it more abundantly.*

A master thief has done his job when he can lead you to an event he has planned. Then while at the event, get you to partake in the festivities, enjoy and even get someone else to enjoy it with you. The devil has done a very good job of stealing and destroying the joy and pleasure of sex and killing the sanctity of marriage today while decimating the unity and oneness of the bond created in marriage.

Too often today, the focus is about how a person can get their needs met rather than how they can meet the needs of others. The Bible paints a beautiful portrait of what love is in 1 Corinthians chapter 13.

> *If I could speak all the languages of earth and of angels, but didn't love others, I would only be a noisy gong or a clanging cymbal. ² If I had the gift of prophecy, and if I understood all of God's secret plans and possessed all knowledge, and if I had such faith that I could move mountains, but didn't love others, I would be nothing. ³ If I gave everything I have to the poor and even sacrificed my body,*

I could boast about it;[a] but if I didn't love others, I would have gained nothing.

[4] Love is patient and kind. Love is not jealous or boastful or proud [5] or rude. It does not demand its own way. It is not irritable, and it keeps no record of being wronged. [6] It does not rejoice about injustice but rejoices whenever the truth wins out. [7] Love never gives up, never loses faith, is always hopeful, and endures through every circumstance.

[8] Prophecy and speaking in unknown languages[b] and special knowledge will become useless. But love will last forever! [9] Now our knowledge is partial and incomplete, and even the gift of prophecy reveals only part of the whole picture! [10] But when the time of perfection comes, these partial things will become useless.

[11] When I was a child, I spoke and thought and reasoned as a child. But when I grew up, I put away childish things. [12] Now we see things imperfectly, like puzzling reflections in a mirror, but then we will see everything with perfect clarity.[c] All that I know now is partial and incomplete, but then I will know everything completely, just as God now knows me completely.

[13] Three things will last forever—faith, hope, and love—and the greatest of these is love.

Love goes beyond emotion or reason to do something for the betterment of another person on their behalf regardless of personal sacrifice because something within you initiated a spark of humanity to connect, as God does. That was His only new command that we love one another. I believe that is why the devil has made it his mission to destroy and tear up so many marriages in this way because unions are so sacred.

After the few dates that I'd gone on didn't work out, I really didn't want to go on anymore. I did want someone in my life, but at the same time, I wanted Patrick back in my life also. But I knew that chapter of my life was over, and I had to move on. However, I didn't want what I saw online or had dated!

I began to focus on what I had learned in DivorceCare classes and was now beginning to teach. I saw the value of the course for people who were going through a divorce or who were separated. These classes were like a roadmap that provided guidance and help to someone trying to navigate unfamiliar waters. I didn't want the distractions of dating someone interfering with me teaching the classes and helping others who needed a friend during a lonely time in their lives.

I was thankful for the classes to keep my mind off dating and the dates that I had gone on since getting a divorce. I had made the mistake of allowing myself to feel lust for one of the men I had gone a date with and been tempted by my desire. I knew that should not have happened because it was outside of marriage, but it was still a weak area in my life as I could only allow God to work in one area of my life at a time without going crazy.

God and the Holy Spirit dealt every so kindly with my heart, knowing that it was in a fragile state from the brokenness of my divorce and the rejection from Patrick. God, spoke through the Holy Spirit to let me know that he only wanted to protect my heart and keep it from getting hurt again. I knew according to His word that the only way to do that was by waiting until God brought the right man into my life and I was married again. Until that time, God showed me that I could continue helping others. That was a task which seemed easier than figuring out what some of the new stuff means on that online dating. I need a dictionary just to understand what the heck they meant between sex, dating, and cybersex!

CHAPTER TEN

Forgiveness

Forgiveness was never hard for me. I always made it a choice to forgive as Christ had forgiven me. After the divorce, I knew that it would be hard to forgive Patrick. My heart had been decimated, and all I wanted to do was cry. But, I knew from the people I had known that I didn't want to live with hatred in my heart and allow it to turn into bitterness against him.

The DivorceCare classes had a lesson on forgiveness, but I had already settled the matter with God. God instructs us in Ephesians 4:31-32,

> Get rid of all bitterness, rage, anger, harsh words, and slander, as well as all types of evil behavior. [32] Instead, be kind to each other, tenderhearted, forgiving one another, just as God through Christ has forgiven you.

According to scientists at John's Hopkins University, chronic anger puts you in a flight or fight mode and changes your heart rate, blood pressure, and immune response. Even scientists have proven that harboring unforgiveness can lead to health problems like increasing the risk of depression, heart disease, and diabetes, among other conditions.

The bible states in Galatians 6:7,

> Be not deceived; God is not mocked: for whatsoever a man soweth, that shall he also reap

People often allow emotions to dictate whether

they forgive or not claiming that it is too hard to forgive. When they are blinded by the truth covered in selfishness, people often see reflections of themselves in the person they do not want to forgive, and the realization of that ugliness is unbearable.

Sometimes people don't want to forgive because they believe forgiving the person is letting them "off the hook" with no consequences for the wrong they did, so they want to hold a grudge and keep the bitterness in their heart. They want to make them pay for the wrong they have done. However, God tells us that He will be our judge and He will be our vindicator for the wrongs people have done to us if we will allow God to handle it. God's timing is perfect, even when we don't think it is.

God wants to give forgiveness to everyone and restore us back to an intimate relationship with the Father where we can learn about His mercy, grace, and unfailing love for us. Unforgiveness is really hate disguised as our own selfishness masking wounded pride. Pride is the battle and struggle within each of us that is the single most significant battle that wages unforgiveness against either ourselves or with others. If we are unable to yield to God and surrender the hurt and wounded parts of the heart we try to guard in our prideful state to show we can take care of ourselves; we doom ourselves to perpetual unfulfilled loneliness.

I learned that there is a peace that God gives in forgiveness that passes all understanding. A peace in forgiveness that calms and soothes the soul.

CHAPTER ELEVEN

Reconciliation

N oah Webster's dictionary defines reconciliation as:

1. The act of reconciling parties at variance; renewal of friendship after disagreement or enmity.

2. In Scripture, reconciliation is the means by which sinners are reconciled and brought into a state of favor with God, after natural estrangement or enmity; the atonement; expiation. Seventy weeks are determined upon thy people and upon thy holy city, to finish the transgression and to make an end of sin, and to make reconciliation for iniquity. Daniel 9:24, Hebrews 2:17.

3. Agreement of things seemingly opposite, different or inconsistent.

After Patrick and I were divorced, I still held onto the hope that we might one day reconcile our marriage. The act of reconciliation is built on a nature of hope and trust in a positive friendship. It is something that must be believed in and wanted, but once a trust has been broken and lost, how do you trust again?

That was the question I had to ask myself every time I saw Patrick and wanted to believe he might be coming to see me for the possibility of reconciliation. I wondered if he might be wondering the same thing too. I think we were like two people dancing around the issue of trying to put together something that was broken which could be repaired but never fixed to be as it was before it was broken. In cases like this, who would want to go back to a state where the fix would require a "disjoint" to repair disharmony in a dysfunctional marriage.

God began to show me that sometimes the blessings He wants to bring us cannot happen until we allow ourselves to let go of the past and surrender to God. I had to let Patrick go, as he had made his decision to leave and not come back. I could not make him come back no matter how much I hoped, just as I could not make him stay when I wished for it the day the judge dissolved our marriage.

Sometimes the pain caused between two people is too much to bear between them. While it is true God can heal a broken heart, give beauty for ashes, bring reconciliation to marriages, and even forget the mistakes of our past when we confess them; people are the ones who have memories that will not forget. We must make a choice to replace the memory with another memory or be consumed with a haunted past that will become a coffin of regrets we then have to dig ourselves out of or become buried in.

I had to allow God to begin a new work in my life and begin to focus on the future. It was hard at first, and I didn't want to think of a future without Patrick in it, but

I had to or be stuck in a perpetual state of repetition that didn't change. I had to start praying again, but this time I prayed in reverse. I prayed that God would help me to not get excited when Patrick called or texted anymore. I knew that I had to allow that hope to fade, just as he had moved on with his life, I too had to move on.

I would have to take the lessons and the truths God showed me from the brokenness of my marriage to learn from them. I also had to ask for the patience to understand the lessons and revelations God was revealing to me during the weeks and months the calls and texts from Patrick began to fade. Then over those weeks and months the calls, texts, and even visits became less and less. The sting and pain of losing a friend I had known became more tolerable with each passing day.

I thanked God that at least Patrick and I parted on good terms, as friends. Even though it felt like I had lost my best friend to death, each day became a little easier, and the sting faded little by little.

While I knew that reconciliation with Patrick would not happen, God showed me that He wanted reconciliation with me. In fact, He sought me out and pursued me because He made me and knew me before I was even born. The bible says in Psalms 139:13-18,

> *13 You made all the delicate, inner parts of my body and knit me together in my mother's womb.*

14 Thank you for making me so wonderfully complex! Your workmanship is marvelous— how well I know it.

15 You watched me as I was being formed in utter seclusion, as I was woven together in the dark of the womb.

16 You saw me before I was born. Every day of my life was recorded in your book. Every moment was laid out before a single day had passed.

17 How precious are your thoughts about me,[b] O God. They cannot be numbered! 18 I can't even count them; they outnumber the grains of sand! And when I wake up, you are still with me!

God was showing me that for the first time in my life I had a relationship with Him now. I had been reconciled with Christ and not just a seat warmer in the church I attended. There was a comfort in knowing that I now had a friend that would be by my side. A friendship that would grow deeper and stronger over time as I got to know Him better, just like you would a friend – just as you would when you reconcile with someone.

CHAPTER TWELVE

Moving On Up With God

Going through the divorce and then going through the DivorceCare classes had made the time pass quickly. It was funny that when the process started, I could recall and even wrote in my journal how I thought this would never end. Now, years have passed, and the sting of losing Patrick had faded.

But, I reconciled with Jesus and began a journey with the Maker and Keeper of my soul. I have given Jesus my heart, and He now is the protector of my heart. It sounded so much easier in my head than walking it out in faith day in and day out, especially when trials came along.

A lot of us have heard of the scriptures from James 1:2-4,

> *2 Dear brothers and sisters,[a] when troubles of any kind come your way, consider it an opportunity for great joy. 3 For you know that when your faith is tested, your endurance has a chance to grow. 4 So let it grow, for when your endurance is fully developed, you will be perfect and complete, needing nothing*

Most people, myself included, generally hate and don't like for bad things to happen. I know that I used to dread it when they would happen to me and then the all too familiar question – "Why me, God?" But God, in his infinite wisdom, began to show me that trials were a good thing, just like James was telling us in the above scriptures.

The trials bring out all the bad things that God and the Holy Spirit need to work on with us so that we may become more like Christ. The Bible tells us that only God knows the heart of a man, which is why we are not to judge another. We have our own problems to work out with God and the Holy Spirit without trying to solve someone else's problems. However, since we don't know the heart of man, we are told to test the spirits and find out what kind of fruit they bear because even if they fool you for a season, eventually a person's true colors and makeup will come out, and you will see what kind of person they truly are.

I began to understand the Christian walk was not only a journey of friendship between Jesus and me but one of growth. The idea of experiencing a friendship and the love Christ offers to me is beyond anything we can comprehend on this Earth. It is almost unfathomable except for the faith to believe.

I believe that is why we struggle a lifetime to press toward perfection, never to achieve it. But for those who make the decision to move on up with God and walk this life with Him, there comes with it a peace in knowing He will always be there to walk with you. A walk that only experience will afford you. No words will convince you. It is in surrender through faith that one can move on up with God in this life and the next or move on in this life alone.

Credits

DivorceCare©, Wake Forest, NC: International Bible Society, 1984
www.churchinitiative.org, www.divorcecare.org

Meyer, Joyce, *Battlefield of the Mind*, (Fenton, Missouri: Hachette Book Group, 1995)
www.joycemeyer.org, www.warnerfaith.com

www.ingramcontent.com/pod-product-compliance
Lightning Source LLC
Chambersburg PA
CBHW071928020426
42331CB00010B/2773